I0059459

THE AUTHORITY GUIDE TO
PERFORMANCE MANAGEMENT

How to build a culture of excellence
in the workplace

GENE JOHNSON

The Authority Guide to Performance Management

How to build a culture of excellence in the workplace
© Gene Johnson

ISBN 978-1-909116-94-8
eISBN 978-1-909116-95-5

Published in 2017 by Authority Guides
authorityguides.co.uk

The right of Gene Johnson to be identified as the author
of this work has been asserted by him in accordance with the
Copyright, Designs and Patents Act 1988.

A CIP record of this book is available from the British Library.

All rights reserved. No part of this book may be reproduced, stored
in a retrieval system, or transmitted in any form or by any means,
electronic, mechanical, photocopying, recording or otherwise,
without the prior written permission of the publisher.

No responsibility for loss occasioned to any person acting or
refraining from action as a result of any material in this publication
can be accepted by the author or publisher.

Contents

"

What we fear doing most is usually what we most need to do.

Ralph Waldo Emerson

"

Introduction

Performance management is one of the most contentious human resources practices within the workplace. It has huge potential to impact positively on the success of an organisation, because it can provide clarity about and information on the direction of a company's business objectives and enhance employee motivation to achieve them. Yet, the negativity surrounding typical performance management systems' 'flawed' processes, inputs and, most notably, performance ratings can seriously detract from any positive outcomes, even to the point of derailment.

With this in mind, employers are taking action to overhaul their performance management systems. The most obvious trend, albeit only among a small number of employers, has been to eliminate performance ratings and simplify processes. However, more successful organisations will look more broadly and focus on ensuring that they are shaping a *performance culture*, where performance excellence is expected and reinforced. For many workplaces, this will involve significant change management. While this will likely involve process changes, it's vital that these are a minor focus and, indeed, that performance management processes are simplified. The main focus should instead be on the core aspects of setting performance expectations (i.e. goal setting), feedback and equitable reward.

This book is about successful performance management through a culture of performance excellence. Specifically, it offers guidance on how to build and shape such a performance culture. It also addresses other relevant aspects, such as clarity around the purposes for conducting performance management, ensuring alignment with strategic business objectives and organisational values, and how to manage the 'mechanics' of performance management processes without over-engineering them.

What is performance management?

Very broadly speaking, performance management can be anything that facilitates or enhances the performance of employees in the workplace. It works to align employee efforts with strategic organisational objectives. In this way, resources can be directed to where they are needed, whether they are basic feedback, development support or performance incentives.

Practically and operationally, performance management usually refers to a system or set of processes that encompasses:

- the setting of individual performance goals between manager and employee
- feedback on and review of goal progress
- reward for goal attainment
- development actions when goal attainment falls short or could be enhanced.

A typical performance process, at least one maintained by larger organisations, looks like this:

Figure 1 Typical performance process

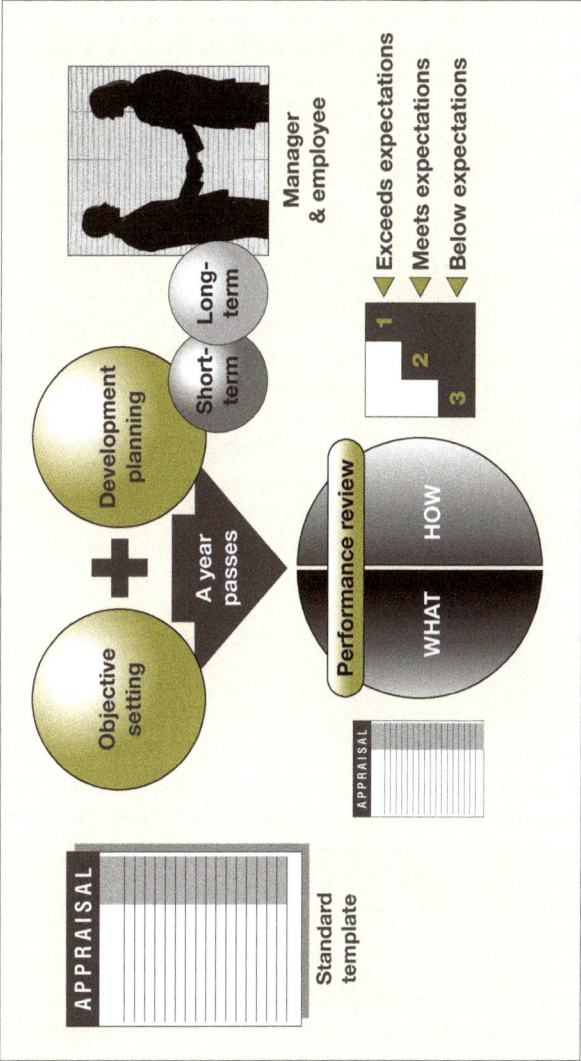

Standard template

APPRAISAL

Objective setting

+

Development planning

A year passes

Short-term

Long-term

Manager & employee

Performance review

WHAT

HOW

APPRAISAL

Exceeds expectations

Meets expectations

Below expectations

1

2

3

A performance cycle typically runs over a year and is quite a formal affair. That is, both manager and employee are required to complete standard forms, documenting, first, plans for the year (performance goals and development objectives) and then meeting later to review progress (usually a year later, sometimes every six months).

Assessment of the employee's performance attainment results in a rating. As processes go, this one is often criticised as an inflexible, administrative juggernaut with little meaning – a 'tick-box exercise'. In organisations with a weak performance culture, this may indeed be true, but not so in cultures of performance excellence. Not to worry, this process can be rectified and transformed as long as two key elements are present: clear expectations (goal setting) and feedback (performance review).

What this book is *not* about

This book is *not* about procedures and forms. It's not one of those 'how to' books. Don't get me wrong: this book offers plenty of models, techniques and tips on what to do. However – and it's a BIG 'however' – without the right culture, such tools will lack effectiveness and *oomph*. To emphasise the point, without the right culture, you'll be running an uphill race, ticking the box, working too hard towards nothing, hitting a brick wall, wasting resources... you get the picture.

This book is about the elements that make up a performance culture. Focus on understanding those elements and how you can improve them in your workplace. Once they're in place, you'll find that you probably have already implemented some of the tools, but they will feel natural and part of 'how things are done' – rather than like add-ons.

It's also worth mentioning that this book is not a 'how to' change management guide. That would take a whole other book to achieve. Rather, as the focus is on building a successful performance culture, this book offers some guidance on how to set up your change process for success. The final chapter on 'bringing about cultural change' provides a framework for understanding the most important aspects of change. For a deeper understanding of change management, you'd be advised to identify a recognisable model and read up on it – you could even get certificated as a change master!

The intended audience for this guide is a 'practitioner' in the workplace. This includes managers of people, leaders of organisations and HR professionals. The common aim for these individuals is that they all want to change the culture of their organisations. The people manager may want to be able to expect excellence from their team and help them grow. The leader may want to increase productivity and quality and help their organisation prosper and grow. The HR professional wants to support both their leaders and people managers in building a performance culture.

How to read this book

You can read this book in one of two ways. The first is to read it from cover to cover, to get an overview of a performance culture. If you're looking for some quick insights, however, the alternative is to read the very next chapter on what a performance culture consists of, then delve into specific chapters. Each chapter concerns one of the individual cultural elements, and you might have a particular interest in one – say, a feedback environment – or you may be aware that you need to work on a particular issue. This book is meant to be that practical.

There are a number of exercises listed in this book for you to use. They are intended to be completed by groups of decision makers and you may want to review them first individually in order to get a heads-up on what the relevant issues may be.

1. The importance of performance management

Simply defined, a performance management culture is one where performance excellence is the norm. A performance culture is built through several important factors:

- A clear and inspiring organisational vision that drives all performance objectives at all levels – organisational values support this vision.
- Clearly communicated expectations about roles, objectives and performance excellence.
- A 'feedback environment' where the offering and seeking of feedback is the norm, in all directions and at all levels.
- Performance distinctions that are equitably rewarded.
- A development and improvement focus, rather than a remedial intent.
- Simple, flexible, and agile performance management processes, allowing easy redirection of employee efforts as objectives and contexts change.
- The 'manager as catalyst': supervisors and managers direct and guide, support and develop, and inspire their staff to do better and grow.

Three essential elements

In addition to the factors listed on the previous page, there are three essential elements that must be present for a culture of performance excellence to operate successfully:

Essential element 1: goal setting

Goal setting is a plan of action designed to achieve an objective. It is an incredibly powerful practice: it motivates through providing direction, challenges staff to persist and stretch, and energises them.

Essential element 2: feedback

Goal setting may be powerful, but it cannot be effective without its partner, feedback. Feedback is both informative (about task progress) and motivational, especially when the feedback is positive and constructive.

Essential element 3: reinforcement

While goal setting and feedback support the achievement of a performance objective, reinforcement is the reward for getting there. In organisational contexts, reinforcement is typically financial, such as a pay rise or bonus. Yet, it could also have nothing to do with money – e.g. praise and recognition ('warm fuzzies') and non-monetary rewards of value to individuals (e.g. promotion, development, time off from work, vouchers).

Figure 2 How the three essential elements work on performance

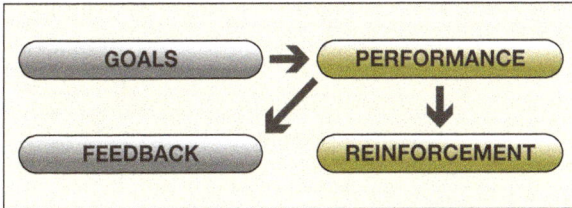

Why performance management may not be successful

Performance management fails within organisations when one or more of the three essential elements is missing or, more typically, is not allowed to operate meaningfully. Although there may be other reasons, either situation usually occurs due to the following:

- Lack of clear performance objectives or too many of them so that they become meaningless.
- Lack of alignment between strategic business objectives and individual goals.
- Poor manager feedback practices or skills, or staff simply not getting feedback regularly enough.
- 'Problems' with ratings – e.g. forced distributions, supervisor-only input, aversion to ratings, poor distinctions between performance levels.
- Budgets that are too limited to adequately reward and make distinctions between staff with different levels of competency.
- Excessive administrative requirements that detract from meaningful performance conversations.

The above flaws have long been the 'hue and cry' or rallying call against performance management. Organisations with strong performance cultures purposefully design their performance management systems to avoid these traps and bugbears. Instead, they maintain a focus on setting core objectives, having meaningful performance conversations and ensuring that great, good and poor performance are equitably distinguished with appropriate rewards (or not...).

Openness and trust

There are two final aspects of a performance culture that must be present: openness and trust. These underlie the three essential elements. Staff have to trust that management are communicating openly and honestly with them at all times and in all matters, including focusing on the right objectives, offering accurate and credible feedback and justifying any performance-related decisions (e.g. financial, promotion).

While complete openness about all details may be limited in some situations (e.g. an impending restructure), managers (and this probably means you...) do have control over communicating what they (you...) do and do not know, can and cannot say. In such an open environment, employees will then proactively ask for feedback from their bosses. Indeed, in some workplaces, feedback provision is employee driven.

Inspiring with a vision and values

Having a clear, inspiring organisational *vision* is the starting point for a performance culture. Employees need to know what to aim for. Imagine striving for excellence, but not really knowing what you were working towards? This isn't just about what a company makes or the service a government department provides; it's not even about how the work is done. Rather, it's an

inspiring vision of *why* the organisation exists. This can be difficult to encapsulate meaningfully in one sentence or paragraph,
but communicated powerfully, it can get your staff enthusias-
tic about and committed to performing, and your customers/
clients eager to buy whatever it is you offer. Part of the challenge is translating an overarching vision so it is equally relevant
across the organisation at all levels and in all departments.

Organisational *values*, whether they are explicitly identified or
implicitly operating, reflect what is important in an organisation.
They dictate common beliefs and what gets done. A strong
vision taps into one more core values, indicating alignment
between what is valued and what the organisation's 'why' is.
A vision not based on a central value or indeed in conflict with
core values is unlikely to be sustained or achieved.

Communicating clear expectations for performance excellence

If you work for an organisation with well-established procedures, such as well-documented job and role descriptions, this
element may seem quite obvious to you. But there are many
organisations that don't provide this level of guidance and
structure – possibly because they haven't felt the need, or even
because their business or work context is so dynamic it may not
be worth the effort. Still, *setting clear expectations* is more than
about writing a job description – at its most basic, it's letting an
individual know what their job is, what they must achieve and
how well they must do it.

Goal setting (essential element 1) is... well, *essential* to setting
clear expectations. There are three aspects to setting goals
effectively:

- Goals should be SMART: Specific, Measurable, Attainable,
  Relevant and Time-bound.

- It's important to aim for a balance of 'what' (results) and 'how' (competencies) in setting goals. Include only the most core and important goals, to ensure a realistic focus.
- Individual goals (and team ones, for that matter) must be aligned with strategic business objectives; this connection has been lost in some workplaces, either due to lack of oversight or poor communication.

Creating a feedback environment

Feedback (essential element 2) is information about how someone is doing on a task or progressing towards a performance goal. A *feedback environment* is a culture in which giving and seeking feedback is expected, encouraged and the norm. Here, feedback flows freely in all directions: not only downwards, but laterally between colleagues and upwards to managers. It should also be requested from clients, customers and service users. So, there are *multiple feedback sources*. Remarkably, employees seek out feedback, rather than waiting for it to be received. Feedback here is typified by its *real-time nature*: it happens in the moment, when it's needed. It's also *constructive*. There is openness and trust, because managers are aware of their staff's performance (i.e. they see it in action or have access to reliable data) or rely upon it from credible others. There is also a good *balance* of feedback, meaning that there's a healthy dose of 'celebrating success'.

Making performance distinctions and rewarding equitably

Workplaces with good performance cultures ensure that different performance levels are appropriately recognised and rewarded. That is, they reward superior performance exponentially more than just satisfactory performance, and they manage

underperformance with remedial efforts or performance discipline as needed. This not only ensures that essential element
3 – reinforcement – is allowed to operate, but it also addresses
people's need for equity and fairness: that different levels of
input (i.e. performance output or quality) deserve different reward levels.

Focusing on development and improvement

Organisations with a performance culture emphasise development and performance improvement over remediation. There's
more focus on 'what could be' rather than fixing what isn't
working.

Development is essential to performance management; it is
how staff learn and improve productivity and performance.
Development activity can be both formal and informal, but there
should always be some sense of structure, including learning objectives, relevant application to the job, reflection and
feedback points. The learning medium has traditionally been
the classroom, but increasingly the benefits of on-the-job or
experience-based development are being recognised.

In addition to developing someone's current role, cultures of
performance excellence provide active support of employees'
career development. Some organisations have standard long-
term career discussions as an element of the regular conversations between managers and staff.

Designing a simple, minimal and agile performance management process

Employers with a strong performance culture of excellence
have *minimal performance management processes*. They
know that the real value derives from meaningful performance

conversations – not from administrative procedures. These organisations also appreciate that the dynamic nature of the current workplace requires *agility* and *flexibility* and that cumbersome procedural requirements would only get in the way.

If you want to change the performance culture of your organisation, you should be careful of simply tinkering with surface-level process matters; any changes must reflect real cultural intent. For example, redesigning a document is very different in intent from no longer requiring any documentation at all. There is no 'magic' formula in terms of simplicity, but you may consider types of ratings, number of rating points, frequency of performance reviews and documentation requirements. You may even decide to eliminate performance ratings, although in no way is this a prerequisite for a performance culture. One factor in deciding that is the ultimate objective of your performance management system (*see* Chapter 2).

Building manager capability: manager as catalyst

Managers – team leaders, supervisors and bosses among others – in organisations with cultures of performance excellence play a very central role. Perhaps this is already obvious, given our previous discussion. It's the manager who has to transmit organisational vision to their team, to translate it meaningfully in the team or group context. It's the manager who has to set clear and strong expectations for performance excellence, including sitting down with staff and helping them arrive at appropriate performance goals. It's the manager who must feedback in real time, proactively offer development and improvement support (including identifying development opportunities) and ensure that different levels of performance are relatively acknowledged and rewarded. This is a huge ask and manager capability will be tested... but performance cultures expect them to rise to the challenge and provide the necessary resources and development.

Organisations viewing their people managers in this way have really got it right. The term 'people manager' suggests that the bulk of their job should be about their people. A common term for this refreshing development is 'manager as coach', in that managers here act more like coaches – inspiring, aligning, growing and helping staff adapt. It's an apt term, but 'manager as catalyst' is even more evocative of a manager transforming their team to reach their potential through all the tools and resources available.

It's worth considering another aspect that managers as a whole will have responsibility for: creating and maintaining the culture of openness and trust. Although they do not have total control over this (executives and senior leadership may exert more of an influence), there are actions they can take to develop such an atmosphere within their own teams. Form follows function.

66

Form follows function.

Louis Sullivan
architect

99

2. Performance management objectives

Before delving into the cultural elements of performance excellence, it's useful for us to first explore why organisations like yours carry out performance management processes. Why? Because performance cultures are clear about the focus of any performance management in place.

In an ideal performance culture, the intent is to drive performance via people. This is done by appealing to their need to excel, their need to develop and grow, their need for more money (if incentives exist) and/or possibly even their need to be part of a team or bigger entity. Of course, to 'drive performance' is a very simplistic concept.

What exactly is your organisation trying to achieve through performance management? What business challenge(s) are you addressing – revenue growth, profit, cost-reductions, staff engagement or something else? If you know this, you can better focus your evaluation and reward efforts.

Many organisations conduct performance management without having a clear sense of purpose. They may insist that it's intended to promote performance, and they may link ratings with bonuses and other decisions. But they haven't consciously thought about what they want to achieve and how they could obtain it through performance management design. Instead, they just blindly follow the somewhat standard practice of other organisations: you set objectives, you review progress at set periods, you start over again.

Decision making versus development

A common theme of different system objectives (when they are clear, that is) is that they relate to decision making of some sort: allocating rewards, identification for promotion, managing poor performance, etc. A contrasting theme is one of development: now that we know your weaknesses, we can focus on supporting you. These represent the extremes in purpose; many organisations may find themselves somewhere in the middle. And, of course, it would be very difficult to imagine an organisation where employment decisions are not reliant on at least some performance data. Yes, tenure plays a part in some organisations – e.g. unionised or government workplaces – but merit and performance will still play some part.

Is a decision-making focus more appropriate for a performance culture? No! Although the explicit link between performance and decision outcomes reflects a desire to reward those making a high impact and thus sends a message to other staff about performance expectations, this is not the only way to motivate. The premise of a development focus is that individuals are motivated by growth. From that perspective, a strong performance message is also possible: 'We expect you to excel. With personal growth, you can excel. We will support your growth and development.'

It's not about performance at any cost

It's worth noting that performance cultures are not about performance at any cost. An overly aggressive approach to business is uni-dimensional in its motivational appeal, potentially alienating staff who might be motivated by more than just money. It also has no respect for people and their contributions, their health and their growth. In addition, there's a great risk that a blinkered focus on performance and only performance might lead to illegal and unethical activities. In the end, you have a toxic environment, which is not sustainable. By contrast, a performance culture aims for the success of both the organisation and its staff, so that each prospers and grows.

Eliminating performance ratings

The trend in some organisations to eliminate performance ratings has been prominent in the business press. Its significance is both in the simplification of performance management processes and the intended reduction in the negativity associated with ratings (e.g. their perceived subjectivity and inequity). Yet, there's the risk that this is simply the newest 'flavour of the month' or organisational fad.

Eliminating ratings is a big, big decision to make. It is not a simple process change. Doing so will not solve all the difficulties with performance management. Indeed, if your organisation doesn't really have a performance culture and gets rid of ratings, it could actually cause more problems than already exist. That is, the absence of the structured rating process and documentation can mean that managers no longer attend to the basics of giving proper feedback and having performance conversations.

Note that being an organisation with a performance culture doesn't necessarily mean *not* having performance ratings; as noted in Chapter 6, every employer measures performance in some way – even if they eliminate performance ratings. What sets those with a performance culture apart is that they are very clear about what they are measuring and why they are measuring it.

One consideration you could make in determining whether you should get rid of ratings is the nature of the work and to what extent it or its outputs are quantifiable. In jobs where you can easily count or measure what gets done or produced, representative ratings may make more sense. But for jobs where it's hard to say what gets done – say, the typical managerial job – and assessment is more qualitative, the omission of performance ratings may seem to make more sense. In this context, a descriptive, constructive narrative by someone's manager is more relevant. However, the narrative must still be used to make decisions – remember, we still have to make bonus decisions, promote staff, etc.

So, even though the rating has gone, it's replaced with another index to make the decision. The risk is that the replacement index will have the same downsides, and if it's left to manager discretion, there's still some sort of rating or ranking that's likely to be even more subjective.

So, there's no easy answer to whether or not you should eliminate your ratings – you simply need to consider the nature of the work, the decisions you expect to make and the risks incurred if you get those wrong. An alternative approach could be to consider how you might simplify the ratings process – in the spirit of ensuring an easier, more agile performance process.

3. Inspiring with a vision and values

Start with a vision

Having a clear, inspiring organisational vision is the starting point for a performance culture. Employees need to know what to aim for.

The *vision statement* is an inspirational, compelling answer to these questions: Why do we exist? What do we hope to achieve or accomplish? What do we aspire to be? What is our mandate? It's essentially your *strategic intent*.

Here are some examples of inspiring vision statements:

- *Oxfam*: 'A just world without poverty'.
- *Human Rights Campaign*: 'A world that achieves fundamental fairness and equality for all'.
- *NASA*: 'To fly what others only imagine'.
- *Amazon*: 'To be Earth's most customer-centric company; to build a place where people can come to find and discover anything they might want to buy online'.
- *Microsoft*: 'To help individuals and businesses realise their full potential'.
- *Google*: 'To provide access to the world's information in one click'.

It's worth repeating: an inspiring vision attempts to answer 'why' an organisation exists. The vision should be 'lived and breathed' day-in and day-out by staff and be compelling enough to motivate them to achieve it.

Don't confuse the vision with detail around 'what' an organisation makes or does or 'how' they do it. A *mission statement* describes how a company will realise and execute its vision. It's the tactics that make the vision a reality.

Core values: why we do what we do

Core values are the important and lasting beliefs or ideals shared within an organisation about what is good or bad, desirable or undesirable. They are 'why we do what we do'. They influence behaviour and attitudes, and serve as broad guidelines in all situations. Values are ends rather than means – what we strive for individually and organisationally. Core values within an organisation help define its culture – if they are really believed, they dictate what gets done and what will be rewarded. An inspirational vision incorporates the most important organisational values, even if only implicitly – e.g. what value do you think Google's vision (*see* page 15) implies?

Existing organisations will have values they operate by, even if they are not explicit. Values tend to be reinforced by the most senior leaders in the workplace, through rewarding certain behaviours both formally and informally, and ignoring and/or penalising other non-preferred behaviours. Desirable organisational values can be identified, with two major caveats as to their sustainability:

1. They must reflect what is really valued and rewarded; if they are 'on paper' only, they will have no impact.

② To make an impact, if the values are currently only aspirational, leaders must 'walk the talk' and reinforce them. This is how organisational change occurs.

Exercise: creating core organisational values

Purpose

To generate a list of the core organisational values that represent what is important to an organisation – that is, what gets rewarded.

Instructions

Step 1 – Organise leader groups

Arrange a group session of no more than 8–10 of your most senior leaders, including your CEO/managing director. Schedule 2–4 hours for this exercise. Depending on the size and complexity of your organisation, you can do this with multiple groups of leaders at the same level and at different levels – indeed, it's highly recommended to do the latter. The more people involved, the more transparent the process and the more likely acceptance of the core values identified.

However, each level of management is likely to have different perspectives on what is important and what gets rewarded. So keep the different levels separate to start with, to prevent less senior managers being afraid of saying in front of their bosses what they see as the current values (or what isn't valued).

From each level, if it is not possible to include all managers due to their number, choose those you think best represent your organisation's core values. You may also want to involve non-managers – again, the more people involved, the more representative the outcome will be. As with managers, include those staff you think best represent the core values.

Step 2 – Brainstorm core values

Present the following questions to your leaders: What is important to our company? What is unique about working here? What gets rewarded?

Each individual writes down the ideas that come to mind, each on its own Post-it® Note. Stop after ten minutes – anything written in this time should reflect the most obvious values to have come to mind. Display the Post-it® Notes on a flip chart or whiteboard so every idea is visible.

If little is generated, 'negate' the question. Ask instead: 'What is our company *not*?' or 'What do similar companies do that our organisation would *never* do?' Phrasing it this way often helps groups come up with fresh ideas.

Note: You can prep your participants prior to the session by asking them to think about values, so they are more easily produced during the group session.

Note: This resulting list should reflect *actual* values. If there are values your organisation aspires to but hasn't yet achieved, you should list these separately. Aspirational values are not currently rewarded or reinforced, and will take a different effort to bring to fruition.

Step 3 – Create a core values list

Sort the Post-it® Notes into piles or groups of similar values. For example, you would combine 'development' and 'challenge'. There may be some values that you cannot yet place; revisit them at the end to see if they now fit somewhere.

At first, don't limit yourself to a maximum number of piles. However, when all the values are sorted, aim for a maximum of eight piles. If you arrive at more than this, look through the piles again to find similarities or even complex multi-dimensional values.

Keep track of the number of individual inputs for each pile, even if repeated. Repetition is a signal of importance or shared thinking.

Step 4 – Define your core values

Read through all the piles and come up with these three components for each one:

1. A key title word

2. A core sentence that represents all the related inputs

3. Specific behavioural statements that reflect the value corporate-wide (later, you may decide to define functional-specific behaviours). For example, here is how the value 'openness' is defined in one organisation:

More of	Positive feedback
	Daring to be open – also when I can't deliver as promised
	Treating everyone with respect
	Encouraging the expression of different views
	Demonstrating respect for decisions that have been made
Less of	Trash-talking decisions I didn't agree with
	Complaining without a constructive alternative
	Criticising others who are not present
	Playing the 'blame game'
	Joking about colleagues

Step 5 – Prioritise your core values (optional)

You may decide that you need to prioritise the values identified. This may be the case if:

- you have too many groups and would like to limit the number of values

- there are clearly more inputs for some piles than others.

You are likely to create some piles that are obviously distinct from others, yet are based on very few inputs. If you decide that these don't reflect what is commonly valued, don't include them.

Step 6 – Integrate results from different leader groups

If different groups have produced their own core values, bring everything together. It is best if someone (such as yourself) first reviews the material and identifies commonalities.

A final leader group of representative managers from different levels and functions, plus some non-managers, should be selected to determine the ultimate list of core values.

Some core values

The number of core values is virtually limitless – here's a small sample. Are there any you think that represent your organisation's values?

Above & beyond	Practicality	Creativity	Innovation
Acceptance	Candour	Teamwork	Integrity
Account-ability	Challenge	Development	Knowledge
Achievement	Client-focus	Diversity	Loyalty
Quality	Collaboration	Efficiency	Safety

Adaptability	Compassion	Empower-ment	Openness
Aggressive	Competitive	Ethical	Ownership
Altruism	Cooperation	Flexibility	Risk-taking
Appreciation	Courage	Happiness	Work-life balance

Top tips

Values-based performance management

Leading with values can help inspire staff to perform better and commit more to employers, because of the motivational 'Why?' One study found that 88% of the employees who were aware of their company's core values said they were more engaged with their work and their employer compared to only 54% of respondents who said they weren't aware of the values.

To help staff appreciate your organisation's core values, integrate them meaningfully into everyday organisational practices and ways of working:

- Include the values in your mission and vision ('Why?') statements.

- Articulate the values in 'how' behaviours (vs. outcomes like productivity or 'what' was achieved) – examples are given for 'openness' on page 19.

- Offer general and functional-specific behaviour examples.

- Ensure that the values get the same attention as outcomes.

- 'Live' the values through leadership by example.

- Teach the values, starting with newcomer orientation and induction and at every other possible opportunity.

Creating or refreshing an organisational vision

When creating your organisational vision, keep these principles in mind:

- Capture the essence of having achieved your end goal, as if you were already successful.

- Focus on the long term: vision is stable over time – the 'end' stays the same – but the 'means' can change and flex. This allows for long-term alignment, while short-term actions can shift direction as needed.

- Aim to inspire through personal action and commitment. This is what inspires employees to take action. It can even attract customers, clients, service users and others to your organisation.

- Keep it short and impactful. The most inspiring vision statements are memorable and concise, although they can be longer. In one analysis of 30 non-profit vision statements, the average number of words used was just under 15.

Determining your strategic intent inspirationally

Your organisation may already have a vision statement. If you don't, or if the existing one is not very inspirational, your objective now is to get at your essential strategic intent. You might even want to 'rework' an overarching vision for a specific department or function so that it becomes meaningful in that context. Start with the question: 'Why are we here?'

You get back what you expect, so set your expectations high.

4. Communicating expectations

Goal setting is one of three essential elements in successful performance management (the other two are feedback and re-inforcement or rewards). It is simply the act of creating a plan to achieve an outcome or objective (the goal). The research on goal setting is some of the most robust in the psychological literature; setting a goal leads to a greater likelihood of achieving it.

GOALS ⎯⎯⎯⎯⟶ PERFORMANCE

We know that goals positively impact work performance by being motivational in four different ways:

1. They provide direction for attention and effort.

2. They have an energising effect so that more challenging goals result in greater work effort than less challenging goals.

3. They enhance persistence – specifically, challenging goals extend an employee's effort.

4. They affect work behaviour indirectly by leading to the use of task-relevant knowledge and strategies.

Specific and challenging goals are more motivational. Specific goals are better than vague 'do your best' goals, which are better than no goals at all. Challenging goals that stretch an individual but are not too difficult are more motivational (and thus achievable) than non-challenging goals. The SMART goal mnemonic reminds us just how detailed goals should be.

SMART principles

Specific	Specific goals provide direction. 'I know I need to sell 10% more widgets this month.'
Measurable	An identifiable output index provides something to aim for and built-in feedback. You (and others) know when it's been achieved. 'That sale just took me over my 10% goal – yippee!!'
Attainable	An attainable goal is challenging but not so difficult it can't be achieved. 'All things considered, I believe I can achieve 10%, but 15% would probably be unrealistic.'
Relevant	A goal needs to be relevant to employees; otherwise there is no personal gain. 'My widget goal relates to my job; I want to sell more, but I'll also personally gain from a higher bonus.'
Time-bound	A time-bound goal sets a deadline, which helps an employee plan how to reach the goal (e.g. by setting milestones). 'I have to reach my goal by the end of the month.'

Exercise: SMART goal setting

Purpose

To help you appreciate the value of SMART goals by apply-ing the discipline to one of your own objectives.

Instructions

Do you think SMART goal setting is easy? Take one of your current work goals and try to improve on it. This should be a goal that you would like to achieve in 12 months or less.

Your basic goal:_____

1. Is it Specific? (Who? What? Where? When? Why?)

2. Is it Measurable? How will you measure progress? (How many? How much?)

3. Is it Attainable? (Can this really happen? Attainable with how much effort? What steps are involved?)

4. Is it Relevant? (How relevant is it to what you do and what you understand to be important? How does it relate to your organisation's vision or strategic objectives?)

5. Is it Time-bound? (Can you set fixed deadlines? What are the deadlines? What milestones should you build in?)

Your goal statement

Now use the information above to write a SMARTer goal statement.

Top tip: goal setting

- *Stay focused.* Limit the number of performance goals to three. You might have sub-goals, but be realistic about what you can achieve.

- *Don't add corporate objectives to individuals' objectives.* It's quite common to attempt to reinforce corporate initiatives like 'diversity and inclusion' with blanket objectives applied to everyone, however, this just adds to the overall number of performance objectives for each individual. While it's true that 'What gets measured, gets done,' these types of corporate objectives can be better addressed through corporate campaigns. Forcing an organisation's objectives on to individuals debases the authenticity of the performance management process.

- *Aim for a balance of 'What?' and 'How?'* Without this, you may achieve a lot in a less-than-constructive manner or exhibit great competency without reaching your goals.

Results and competencies

What you have to achieve in your job is what gets measured in performance management. Performance measures fall into two categories:

1. *Results/objectives:* The goods and services produced by an employee, often measured by performance objectives ('What?')

2. *Behaviours/competencies:* The means by which you achieve your 'What?'s – i.e. the behaviours and values demonstrated during the process ('How?'). See *Top tip* on the next page for examples.

Figure 3 Performance objectives – the 'What?'s

Timeliness	**Quality**
Timeframe to complete work	How *well* work is performed
• Responds to requests within 24 hours	• 25% improvement in client satisfaction
• Provide financial reports on quarterly basis	• Produces reports requiring no revisions

Quantity	**Financial metrics**
How *much* work is performed	Efficient use of funds, revenues, profits and savings
• Responds to 95% of requests	• Achieved a 15% saving on last year's budget
• Wins two new accounts a month	• Increased revenue by 4%

Top tip: identifying competencies

When considering job-relevant behaviours or competencies, break them down into *KSAOs* for easier understanding:

- 'Knowledge' consists of facts or information that can be learned through formal education, training or specific experience – e.g. engineering knowledge.

- 'Skills' relate to practised acts, such as typing efficiency; these may be easily learned or learned over time.

- 'Ability' refers to a stable capacity, such as intelligence or mechanical ability; abilities tend to be viewed as more difficult to learn, if at all.

- 'Other characteristics' include personality variables, values, interests, training and experience.

It's important to require both 'What?' and 'How?' because, as mentioned before, what gets measured is what gets done. Employers who emphasise only what gets done are at risk of ignoring vital 'How?' behaviours such as customer service and teamwork – e.g. a good product offered with poor customer service. Conversely, although much less common, the provision of great service ('How?') supporting a poorly made product ('What?') would not be sustainable. It's also worth pointing out that 'How?' behaviours can reflect core values.

Cascading strategic objectives

The cascading of strategic business objectives down through an organisation looks easier than it is. Organisational goals can be too lofty, so that the connection with other goals may not always be obvious. The challenge is to ensure that all individuals are aware of how their jobs and objectives contribute to a specific strategic objective, no matter what level of the organisation or functional role they are in.

There is no magic wand or miracle tool to make this happen. The communication power of a supervisor or manager to paint an inspirational picture of where their team fits into the bigger picture is vital. A senior leader at the United Nations once told me about a journey she had made with her personal driver, and how, during it, she had been able to connect his job – which was simply driving her and other professional staff to meetings – to the overall mandate of that organisation, which was to bring peace and prosperity to the world!

5. Creating a feedback environment

In the last chapter, we identified goal setting as an essential element for successful performance management. There is one caveat: for goal setting to work, employees must have knowledge of their progress – i.e. feedback. So the marriage of feedback with goal setting is essential.

The value of feedback is two-fold:

- It's informative and provides direction – that is, it lets the person know how well they have performed.

- It can be motivational, especially if it is positive.

Figure 4 The role of goal setting and feedback in impacting performance

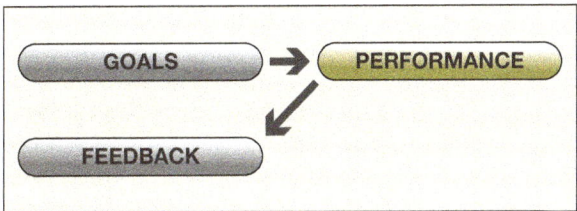

Real-time feedback

For feedback to be most effective, it should be concurrent with the performance or behaviour it relates to. This is known as *real-time feedback*. This necessary time connection is rooted in basic psychology. According to contingency theory, for feedback to have an impact, it must occur at the same time (or very near to) the original action or behaviour; otherwise the connection may be lost. Here's a very simple metaphor: imagine you touched a hot stove, but didn't experience any pain until an hour later. How would you know where the pain came from? Chances are, you might just touch that hot stove again...

Top tip: teachable moments

Real-time feedback has the potential to create a myriad of valuable teachable moments. The vast majority of constructive feedback opportunities are when a misunderstanding occurs, something doesn't go to plan or there's a problem to solve. Real-time feedback is informal, 'in the moment', not an end-of-year performance review. So any feedback is pertinent to the issue at hand, not a review or summary of performance to date. Keep a lookout for opportunities to feedback 'in the moment' and create a teachable moment.

Constructive feedback

Constructive feedback is information-specific and issue-focused, and is based on observations of behaviour or performance. This means that it is not general feedback – for example, 'That was good.' Rather, it should be specific – for instance, 'I liked how you used visuals in your presentation. They really built up a picture for me.' Behavioural observations are descriptive, not evaluative or interpretative: notice the distinction between 'That was very good' and 'You used a great deal of jargon that the audience didn't know. For example, you referred to TLAs three times.'

Constructive feedback can be positive or negative. If you are critiquing the other person's performance, first describe what was poor or ineffective, so it's clear what behaviour needs changing. Then provide a descriptive example of what would be good, to act as a comparison or benchmark. This makes it crystal clear what is expected, as well as providing a goal to aim for.

Even if you are praising performance, you should still describe what was good. This is useful information, and it also enables the other person to repeat the effective behaviour.

Here are some samples of feedback, both bad and good.

Examples: unconstructive vs. constructive feedback

Unconstructive feedback	Constructive feedback
I don't think you're capable of undertaking this level of project.	You'll need to master the following tasks before we assign you this duty.
I've read your report and I expected something more polished given your level of experience in this domain.	I'd like to see some more technical background in section 1, and want you to refine the recommendations so that they're more specific about deadlines and budget.
You've got to be the laziest person on the team.	You've missed the last three deadlines by over a week.

Exercise: asking for constructive feedback

Purpose

To help you practise asking for constructive feedback, so you become more familiar with offering it in turn.

Instructions

While it can be challenging to provide constructive feedback, receiving it ourselves can make us more aware of its impact and value.

Ask for feedback about a recent performance – perhaps a presentation you have given or a meeting you facilitated. If the reply is general or vague, ask the person for more specific details about what you did or did not do well. Then ask what you could do to improve, or ask what a benchmark for good would look like.

Once you have been on the receiving end of 'new and improved' feedback, consider how you can then apply the same principles to someone else. Offer specific, behavioural feedback to someone you have observed doing something in the course of their job.

Top tip: focus on behaviour, not the person

It's important to direct feedback at behaviour, not at someone's beliefs, values or identity. Implying that there is something wrong with a person can be threatening and hit their self-esteem hard. In addition, people may reject your feedback if it is different from their own self-perception.

Instead, address the behaviour that has to change. For example, stating, 'The language you used with your colleague was not professional' is likely to be better received than 'You are crude'.

Alternatives to traditional feedback

Future-focused 'coaching' or feedback

By centring on what the person is working on now or in the near future (e.g. this week), feedback is offered through suggestions about how to work differently, rather than critiquing what has gone before. In practice, this method is a combination of feedback and coaching. Typical future-focused statements include:

- 'You may want to try...'
- 'I would suggest...'
- 'Have you thought about...?'
- 'You may want to think about...'
- 'What would happen if...?'

A scenario might play out like this:

Sharon asked a new graduate to take minutes at the team meeting. What he returned to her was a set of garbled notes.

Rather than asking him why he hadn't taken good minutes, Sharon said: 'I noticed that the minutes you took don't fully represent what was covered in the meeting. I'd like you to take them at the next meeting. What can I do to support you? You may want to try...'

Example: future-focused 'check-ins' at Deloitte

Deloitte, a major consulting and accountancy firm, recently transformed their performance management system so that it became more of an on-going business process rather than just a static annual event.

The core of the process is the check-in, which occurs at least once a week with each team member. The employees initiate the discussions, and the focus is on performance in the near future. Supervisors structure the sessions with questions like this: What are you working on this week? What are your priorities? How can I help you achieve them?

Viewed as coaching sessions, attention is on what the employee should be focusing on during the following week, what they might try to do differently and what support is needed. The supervisor's support and guidance will depend on the employee's strengths, skill levels and experience. This coaching role of the boss is not viewed as an add-on, but as part of their actual day-to-day work as a supervisor.

Strengths-based feedback

Another alternative to the traditional variety is strengths-based feedback. This approach is a reaction to performance management processes being based on a 'deficit model', where a person's area of weakness is their greatest area of opportunity. In contrast, a strengths-based approach assumes that progress towards performance excellence is a function of building on someone's strengths. In this type of performance appraisal, the aim is to identify, appreciate and develop the employee's qualities and to focus on how they can better utilise them. This approach derives from 'appreciative enquiry', which emphasises what works, instead of focusing on fixing what's wrong.

A strengths-based approach does not mean that problematic performance is not addressed or that feedback can only be artificially positive. It does, however, mean that an effort needs to be made to discover the unique qualities of employees and to maximise the opportunity for them to carry out work activities that play to their strengths. Also, weaknesses are not ignored, but managed by finding someone else to do the tasks that someone does poorly or by reducing a weakness to an acceptable level of performance.

Although thorough studies comparing the effectiveness of traditional and strengths-based feedback have not been conducted, there is some support for focusing on employee strengths and talents. It appears that strengths provide a better starting point to build from than weaknesses, as staff are then more open to listening to feedback and development. In one study, a performance management approach that stimulated the use of strengths led to much bigger increases in personal growth compared with one that stimulated development in the area of individual deficiencies. Moreover, working on strengths appears to enhance self-confidence, success expectations, perseverance and resilience in coping with setbacks.

Finally, employees who perceive organisational support for focusing on what they do well become more confident and engaged and, as a result, display higher levels of proactive behaviour and performance and lower levels of absenteeism.

Reflected best self-feedback (RBSF)

This is one kind of strengths-based approach to performance management and development. Another name for this is the *feed-forward interview*. The format asks employees to seek out stories about times they were at their best and made meaningful contributions. These stories are gathered from their friends, family, current and former co-workers, supervisors and subordinates (10–20 in total so they are representative). They are used to compose a 'portrait' of the employee's strengths and talents. From this, a person identifies the settings, relationships and tasks that allow them to be 'at their best' and the actions that will allow them to be their 'best selves' more often. As noted earlier, positive outcomes have resulted from this kind of feedback.

Praise and recognition

Praise and recognition are under-used. The power of a sincere 'pat on the back' or simple 'thank you' can be massive – it acknowledges input and contribution. Even more meaningful is informative, constructive positive feedback – e.g. 'What I really liked about your sales pitch was... If you wanted to improve it, you could...'

Time and time again, workplace surveys tell us that managers overestimate the importance of money to staff, including monetary rewards. One of the surveys looked at the value of 65 potential incentives to motivate staff. Four out of the top five rewards ranked by employees as the most motivating related to praise and recognition:

- Personally congratulating them for a job well done.
- Writing a personal note to them for good performance.
- Publicly recognising them for good performance.
- Holding morale-building meetings with the team or department to celebrate success.

For real-time feedback, give feedback as fits the situation. Keep in mind that not enough good performance is 'caught' and praised, so always look for opportunities to do so. A ratio of 3–4:1 is recommended: for every time negative feedback is communicated, you should find at least three or four opportunities to praise something good in the same employee.

Top tip: provide a balance of positive and negative feedback

A common feedback approach is the *feedback sandwich*. Here, you start with a positive, then introduce constructive feedback, and then finish on a positive note. Proceed with caution using this model, because it can send a message that the outer positive feedback is meaningless and is masking the meat of the matter: the negative feedback. This approach is probably best used for a regular review meeting, where a summary of performance over time is expected.

Feedback usefulness and credibility

Employees want useful and credible feedback. *Feedback usefulness* means that it should be relevant to them and their job. Constructive feedback should address any concerns with that. *Feedback credibility* refers to the accuracy and quality of the feedback – that is, has the feedback provider actually seen the employee perform or seen their work outcomes?

A common complaint is that supervisors don't always see what their staff are doing. In the end, feedback is best sought from the individual or role with the most intimate familiarity or knowledge of the employee's performance. This will vary depending on what is being measured (*see* Top tips on the next page).

Top tip: feedback source suitability depends...

Where feedback is best sourced	To assess...
Supervisor	What gets done/outputs – because supervisors will have sight of this
Peers	How work gets done – because peers most often see how each other works
Employees	What impacts them most – leadership, communication skills, feedback giving and development focus
Customers	Customer service, timeliness, quality and usefulness of outputs and/or services

Exercise: celebrating success

Purpose

To help get you into a mindset of regularly offering praise and celebrating success.

Instructions

Take this in two steps. First, at the individual level, identify positive performance or behaviour for each of your team. In the next week, approach each team member and offer some positive, constructive feedback.

Second, identify a success or achievement in your work arena, the responsibility of either an individual or the entire team. Draft constructive, positive feedback, publicly praise the efforts and offer some type of motivational reward if possible. Consider how you might regularly celebrate success.

360-feedback

360-feedback is the use of multi-source feedback for purely developmental purposes. As a circle encompasses 360 degrees, input from diverse sources (self, supervisor, peers, colleagues, clients, others) is meant to offer a similarly comprehensive scope of feedback. A 360-tool typically comprises a competency-based series of questions to be rated plus comment boxes, although quantitative ratings are not essential.

This all-rounder feedback can provide rich, meaningful data if it is taken seriously by both the assessed and the assessors. The employee must be open to including a wide range of potential input from both their champions and their potential critics. It's also essential that they are open to receiving the feedback and acting on it. Feedback givers must be open to considering the employee's competencies carefully and offering useful and balanced text comments.

However, a common difficulty with 360-feedback tools is the use of competency models that are applied to *all* staff, meaning that a sizeable proportion of items may not apply to each person. Also, the process can be quite burdensome, so it's likely that not all staff requested to provide feedback will do so or do so carefully.

Top tip: interpreting 360-feedback

If you're being assessed via 360-feedback, to get the most out of the feedback report *don't* try to take it all in and address every result. You may find that some findings don't have much meaning for you. So, start with an initial skim read and then read through it again.

Look for three key take-aways. One of these might be a competency area where you have rated yourself most differently from others as a whole. It could include results that resonate with your own understanding of your development needs. Without ignoring what might be important (i.e. don't read the report with blinders on), take away what has meaning for you. Once you have identified your three areas, discuss them and the report with your boss. You could also do the same with your team – it's an honest way to build trust and open communication.

Incorporating social media

A relatively recent trend is to use social media to gather feedback from colleagues and customers. This is known as *social performance management (SPM)*, also known as *crowd-sourcing*. Using social media platforms like Facebook and LinkedIn, or even directly through client surveys, organisations receive feedback about staff. They then stream the feedback and 'recognitions' live on large screens throughout their facilities, making the process spontaneous and interactive. In essence, this is real-time feedback. Managers and employees can also establish and share goals with each other and track progress in real time. The process resembles a conversation rather than capturing records after the fact, with the benefit of capturing that conversation on record.

It is worth noting that SPM is typically not an open forum for criticism; the public feedback is all about recognition. Any 'constructive' feedback is viewed as personal and shared only with the employee. Also, an employee's performance towards goals is visible only to relevant individuals who the manager and employee have agreed on in advance (generally team members).

This is a relatively new arena with no evaluative research. You might question, how meaningful is a performance culture in terms of openness if 'constructive' feedback is offline?

6. Making performance rewarding

The third and final essential element in a performance culture is *reinforcement*. While goal setting and feedback are supports in achieving a performance objective, reinforcement is the reward for success. *Reinforcement theory* states that a positive reinforcement of an action will cause it to repeat (whereas negative consequences will make that less likely). So responses that produce rewards will be repeated – it's that simple. Performance management systems rely on rewards to increase desired behaviour, such as productivity and quality work.

Figure 5 The three essential elements and their relationship with performance

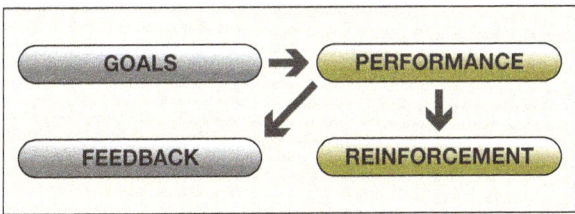

Of course, the reward has to be of some value to the person. We usually think of a reward as money because that's the one thing most people believe they can never have enough of. And from a sceptical point of view, we human beings are 'economic animals': money can give us other things we value.

However, we are also complex animals, so money isn't our only motivator. Rewards can also be non-monetary. The most basic rewards are praise and recognition (*see* Chapter 5); they tend to double-up as both feedback and reward. Other rewards might have an indirect monetary value, such as a promotion, time off from work or gift cards. Some rewards might be valued for different reasons, which means that they might not be equally valued by all. Take employee learning and development as an example. Some staff will see it as a reward because they have a desire to grow, whereas others will see it as an inauthentic gesture – like giving a bag of sweets to someone who works for a sweets manufacturer.

Challenges in connecting performance with reinforcement

If goals are clear and challenging, feedback is accurate and meaningful and the reward is appropriate to the level of per-formance – these three elements will result in effective per-formance management. With these conditions, staff will be motivated to perform to their best and commit themselves to their jobs and employer. However, these perfect conditions rarely exist.

A core difficulty is with the relationship between performance and reinforcement. Let's start with performance. To do this, we also have to address performance's proxy, the *performance rating*. There are a myriad of issues in measuring performance and assigning ratings, depending on the job.

Here is just a sample:

- What are the best indices of performance? Just how objective are these measures? This is known as the *criterion problem*.

- If performance can't be measured objectively (e.g. number of widgets produced), who should provide input? An employee could say, 'How much do "they" really know about what I do or produce? How confident can I be that "they" are not being too subjective?' (*See* Chapter 5 on page 12.)

- What proportion of 'What?' and 'How?' should be reflected in a rating?

- What about the 'politics' involved in determining ratings in the workplace? How transparent is the process of deciding a rating?

What's in a performance rating?

The 'politics' of determining performance ratings is a real issue, in terms of both organisational politics and unconscious feelings and opinions. While there should be a direct relationship between performance and an assigned rating – that is, actual performance should dictate the rating – a host of factors that don't relate to actual performance can determine a rating:

- Previous rating: is it okay to give the same person the top rating again – should it be shared out?

- Purpose of rating: is it for decision-making or for developmental purposes? (Remember from Chapter 2 that these two tend to be the dominant reasons for conducting performance management.)

- Relationship with supervisor.

- Supervisor's rating skill.

- Supervisor's bias: race, gender, etc.

- Organisational politics.
- Salary level: does the person already make 'enough' money?
- Budget: money available.
- 'Criterion problem'.

There are then issues with reinforcement and reward. A common difficulty is limited budget, with only so much money to go around. This means that either only a few people get a reward (which, in theory, makes sense if the best performers are rewarded, but it can upset 'average' performers) or everybody gets a thin slice, so most employees feel under-rewarded. This leads to another common issue: performance distinctions are not obvious enough – that is, the best performers don't receive significantly more than everyone else and the poorest performers aren't disciplined.

When people perceive that rewards are not proportional to their input (not only performance, but also tenure, experience, education and so on) compared to their colleagues, they experience feelings of *inequity*. Inequity is a sense of unfairness, leading to dissatisfaction and lower performance, among other negative outcomes.

Making performance distinctions

Making valid and clear performance distinctions between 'superstar', 'average' and 'poor' performers is vital to the success of effective performance management. Organisations with performance cultures strive to do this, aiming to identify the very best performers and give them top ratings and/or reward them significantly more than everyone else.

If you speak to managers in a workplace, many will say: even without performance ratings, they know who their truly superb performers are. They stand out head and shoulders above the rest. Various studies in different industries have revealed that high performers outshine average colleagues by a long chalk. One such study by Herman Aguinis & Ernest O'Boyle, involving over 600,000 people, estimated that high performers can deliver 400% more productivity than the average performer.

High performers know their 'street value'; they want to be recognised for their performance and see that distinctions are made between them and others. It's important, therefore, to appreciate that strong performers are attracted to organisations that recognise individual contributions differentially. Specifically, they prefer employers who have a reputation for pay-for-performance over fixed-salary compensation systems, which emphasise praise and recognition for individual accomplishment and which offer fast-track promotion for top performers. This also means that star performers will abandon employers who do not differentially reward exceptional performance.

Equity and fairness concepts

It may be illuminating to know that weaker performers will also leave employers who strongly reward high performance, but are more likely to stay when pay-for-performance differentiation is weak.

High performers who perceive that they are rewarded fairly compared to others who don't perform as well should thus experience equity. *Distributive justice* is the term used to refer to such perceptions about fairness of how much of something is received (e.g. a monetary reward or a rating).

Unfortunately, due to the problems inherent in performance measurement and ratings, less stellar performers may experience inequity – remember, we are economic animals so can easily justify that we deserve a higher rating or more money. However, there is a solution that organisations with a performance culture can usefully employ: they can build up perceived *procedural justice* as to how the decision to assign ratings and/or dole out rewards was made. Perceptions of procedural justice are influenced by a number of factors, including:

· transparency in how the decision was made

· whether relevance of input was taken into account

· whether the person's performance or work outcome was observable

· voice – the sense that the employee was heard and able to provide input

· opportunity to appeal the decision

· consistency of administration regarding any process

· feedback timeliness and meaningfulness.

Managers can also ensure that they create perceived *interpersonal justice*. This relates to the interaction between manager and employee in feedback mode or when learning of rating or reward decisions. Aspects of this form of perception include honest communication and being treated with respect and warmth.

Exercise: building procedural justice

Purpose

To help you prepare a fair justification for a performance rating or performance-related decision.

Instructions

Consider an employee who was not happy with their performance rating. Using the factors listed above, how can you bolster their sense of procedural justice in the way the decision was made?

Alternatively, justify the rating given to a high performer.

Managing underperformance

In the previous section, we wanted to ensure that star performers were clearly singled out for top ratings and rewards compared to satisfactory performers. Effective performance distinctions also mean that we need to deal appropriately with those on the other side of the coin, our poor performers.

Both organisations and managers tend to shy away from effectively addressing performance problems. Partly, this is due to a reluctance to give negative feedback directly; nobody wants to deliver bad news, but it's even harder if the other party isn't open to listening. To some extent, this is due to the perceived difficulty in some organisations to battle against a cumbersome performance management system and win.

Employers with performance cultures systematically and proactively manage underperformance. They don't cut any corners – they follow what are viewed as procedurally fair guidelines on communication about poor performance and the issuing of warning notices. They clearly communicate their performance expectations upfront, they attend to any performance concerns before it gets too late, and they offer support to rectify and improve performance.

Action–impact model

In managing someone's underperformance, keep the focus on behaviour. Because the situation can be serious, add two elements to basic feedback: the impact of the employee's behaviour and the consequences to them of not rectifying their behaviour or performance – hence, the approach is referred to as the 'Action-impact model'.

You will typically address two types of underperformance: consistently poor performance and behavioural issues. Although the language may change slightly for each type, the three-prong focus remains the same, as the sample dialogue below shows:

Consistently poor performance	1. 'Your performance has been...'
	2. 'The impact is that you are not meeting your targets...'
	3. If it doesn't improve by X, then the consequences are...'
Behavioural issues	1. 'When you do X...'
	2. 'It makes me/others feel [add relevant adjective(s)]. It affects [add relevant noun(s)]. It [add relevant verb]...'
	3. What I need you to do is...'

Making decisions without performance ratings

One of the complications of eliminating performance ratings is how performance-related decisions are then made. Notwithstanding the significant downsides of ratings, they do provide an objective indicator of performance (at least that's the intention) on which to base decisions such as pay rises and bonuses, promotions, entry to high-potential programmes, development activities and even the decision to terminate an employee's contract (after the appropriate disciplinary procedures have been enacted, of course).

As noted in Chapter 2, the elimination of ratings does not mean that there are no data points in use. An organisation may have eliminated a rating as part of the annual review (and possibly also done away with the annual review itself), but it is likely to have replaced it with something else. The simple problem is:

you can't make a performance-based decision without some index. So all organisations rate their staff, but possibly in different ways.

A survey – by Gerald Ledford and colleagues – of reward allocation methods for firms that were no longer using ratings revealed that the most common approach by far was *manager discretion* – say, in apportioning bonuses, pay rises and the like within a given budget. The problem is, how were they doing it? Were they systematically collecting performance information throughout the year? Were they objectively assessing this information?

Remember, we humans are economic animals and cut corners when we can. Managers are no different. Performance management bureaucracy was initially put in place because of the seeming inability of managers to be objective and fair in assigning ratings and deciding rewards. The first evaluations of employers that were carried out without using ratings confirmed these fears. Without ratings, managers resorted to doing less and doing it more poorly – they failed to set expectations appropriately, hold clear performance and development conversations and provide appropriate rewards and recognition. This had immediate repercussions for staff dissatisfaction. Of course, this would be in workplaces lacking a true performance culture – where, without the structure of ratings, there was no other support for performance excellence.

Calibration sessions are another somewhat common alternative to ratings. Managers discuss qualitative or narrative feedback and attempt to make some sense of the performance levels described, using qualitative benchmarks. If the input is purely text-based, this is the closest in practice to no ratings at all. The sessions are conducted across teams and within departments and divisions, to ensure some equity. It can be quite a cumbersome process; imagine trying to equate apples and oranges and then rank them – although the ranking still introduces a quantitative element.

Two other alternatives are *employee rankings* and *shadow ratings*. Although the annual review rating may have been eliminated, there may still be ratings generated during, say, talent reviews and a rating made during compensation calibration sessions, to give specific examples. In order to distribute money or decide who to promote, employees have to be compared and rated/ranked. Here's an example of how it works:

Bob has to apportion bonus payments to staff based upon two performance criteria: project completion and client feedback. He assesses the performance information and arrives at a rating or ranking based on both quantitative and qualitative data; the top-ranked staff member receives the biggest bonus. So, there are still employee rankings, even if they may be referred to as 'unofficial'. It's quite rare for such rankings to be communicated to staff, so they are in essence 'shadow ratings' – they don't officially exist, but they are there – and the risk is that staff will hear about them through the 'grapevine' and perceive them negatively.

How would organisations with a true performance culture approach this situation? First, even if they opt to 'eliminate' ratings, they do not shy away from constructive feedback that offers individuals useful information about where they stand in relation to performance goals. This might include some index or multiple indices. Performance cultures have clear performance expectations, and one way to let people know how well they are doing is to assess them against a benchmark. Second, whichever index is used would be openly and honestly communicated to staff. There would be no shadow ratings.

7. Focusing on development and improvement

Development is the acquisition or refinement of skills and knowledge, including job mastery (doing your job) and professional development (competencies that may extend beyond the scope of your current job). The most common approach to work-related development is the *70-20-10 model*. The model derives from research done on expatriate executives in the 1980s. The original findings by Morgan McCall, Mike Lombardo and Ann Morrison revealed that these successful leaders learned predominantly from their assignments (73%) and less so from other people (18%) and from formal classroom situations (6%). Over time, the model has evolved to suggest how development *should* occur proportionally.

On-the-job (OTJ) development

This can be the most potent form of development because it is relevant, meaningful and *in the moment*. In cultures of performance excellence, OTJ development is a given and the first consideration for development. The job itself will determine the type of development (*see* the table below). The risk in an organisation that doesn't really value development is that OTJ development becomes a stressful 'figure it out for yourself' experience. While there are some hardy and resilient souls who will be energised by this, many will not and so will miss any learning.

Role	Example of OTJ development
Assembly operator	Stands by a colleague and observes how a task is completed, followed by doing the task herself
Administrator	Learns how to organise an event by shadowing the current organiser, including taking on some tasks himself and reporting back for progress checks
Sales manager	Does a secondment in a different sales department to become familiar with products
High-potential middle manager	Is assigned to a role in an emerging country, to be exposed to the challenges there

Classroom training

This is the usual 'go to' option in many organisations. No longer just the traditional classroom set-up, this form of development now covers a wide range: interactive sessions, online video-conferencing, action learning sets, MOOCs (massively open online communities), vestibule training (off-site skills building, usually using machinery or technology) and so on.

Advocates maintain that the classroom format and its various options allow the time and space outside of the working day to dedicate to development (especially when compared to new training technologies, such as digital training, which can be carried out on your own computer but is likely to be disrupted by the day job). For some types of learning, it can be the most effective – such as skill building or work practice that would result in some cost or risk if a mistake were made in the actual job, or where analysis, reflection and/or discussion among peers adds value. In a performance culture, this type of training has a very precisely defined role: it offers development away from the job when it cannot be experienced on the job. As such, it should constitute a minority of overall development opportunities.

It may be a hard sell to staff, especially professionals and managers, that classroom training is not an automatic development option. In performance cultures, the approach to OTJ development would be structured just enough (i.e. not over-engineered) that it is viewed as an identified opportunity with expected learning outcomes.

Learning through others

This has a core role in a performance culture. Although the current 70-20-10 model usually considers this coaching, the original model referred primarily to 'your boss'. Both are still relevant in a performance culture. Coaching skills can be developed at any level of staff, so not only can managers coach their staff (and others) but peer coaching can also become the norm. The 'boss' has a tremendous opportunity to support staff in their development: providing on-the-job opportunities for development, offering feedback and coaching, expecting excellence, inspiring with vision and role modelling. Chapter 9 discusses more extensively how a boss can transform their employees into exceptional performers.

Structuring development activities

If it's not already obvious, development in a performance culture is a serious matter. You don't just go off to be 'developed' and then return to work. First, there's preparation for the development and, on return to the job, you need to consider how best to apply what's been learned. This is a must-do for all development experiences, whether they are formal (like the classroom) or informal (usually OTJ development). Indeed, in performance cultures, 'informal' OTJ development is edging more towards the formal end of the continuum, to ensure that time and any resources are well invested.

Here's how a development experience could be structured for an employee:

1. *Know what needs to be developed.* Typically, this will emerge from discussions with your boss and a common understanding of your strengths and development needs, based on job performance to date.

   Identify a development opportunity – i.e. some OTJ experience. There are potentially rich development opportunities close to home, in your current job, in a lateral role or in an aspirational role (*see Top tip on page 56*). This may relate to a needed experience or competency development.

2. *Target a learning objective.* How will this experience develop you? What do you want to achieve? Of course, this objective should be SMART (*see page 5*).

3. *Test the objective.* Will it challenge and stretch you? Will it take you enough out of your comfort zone to help you improve your performance or progress in some way, but not so much that you'll find it impossible to achieve or too stressful?

④ *Prepare for the experience and gather support.* This includes identifying any feedback points and who will feedback to you. Are there any milestones with objective data that will indicate how well you are doing? How will the feedback giver know this? Ask the most appropriate person to feed back – your boss, a colleague or anyone else who might see you in action or observe your outputs.

⑤ *Reflect on the experience*, at relevant milestones and on completion. What have you achieved? Now what is your next development need?

Reflection is an essential component of true development and learning. To fully benefit from a development experience, you must work through the complete learning cycle (*see* below).

Figure 6 Learning cycle

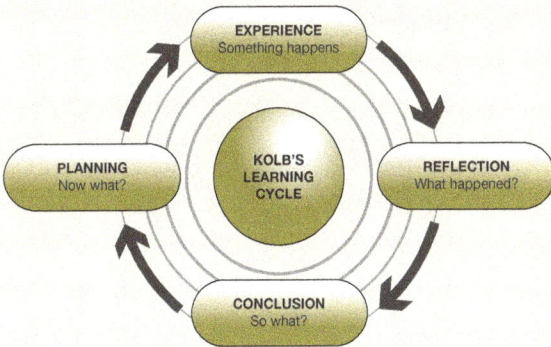

Too often, however, people prefer a particular element or style of learning. For example, some of us like to 'do' and 'act', but then don't take the time to reflect and come to conclusions about what's happened. Some of us like to ponder and reflect, but not actually 'do'.

Example: working through the learning cycle

Bob has identified that he needs to develop his presentation skills. He has had classroom training for this already, so what he needs now is practice.

He has discovered a local competition where people do TED-style talks. He competes and gets to present (*experience*). Pondering how it went (*reflection*), Bob works through the feedback and finds that his humour was effective and his graphics were well received ('Wow, that picture was worth 1,000 words!'), but he had spoken too quickly and given too much detail.

Looking for some common themes (*conclusion*), Bob concludes that he has some performance anxiety, which causes him to ramble and rush. He decides that he needs to work on becoming more relaxed. He decides to learn some mindfulness techniques over the next month and then present again to the same group (*planning*).

Top tip: 'mining' a job for development opportunities

Too often we neglect the development opportunities around us. To identify such opportunities specific to your role, you can 'mine' your job in a search for possible experiences.

The process is deceptively simple and doesn't require complex tools or forms. You simply draw a vertical line and write 'Current job' at the bottom of the line and 'Next job' – your next/aspirational role – at the top. In between the two, consider the tasks, projects and roles that would be involved in getting you to the top (*see* Figure 7 for an example).

This does require knowledge of the required KSAOs (*see* page 27) and experience for both roles (*see* 'Structuring development activities' on page 54 – preparation is key).

Start asking yourself some questions: What are you currently doing that relates to the next role? Is there a common KSAO or task? What new task or project could you take on that will progress your development towards the next role? The new experiences you identify will usually be related in some way to your current experience and competency. You might consider some 'left field' experiences, but the further away they are from your current state of play, the less likely you are to experience them at this point.

Figure 7 An example of 'mining' a job

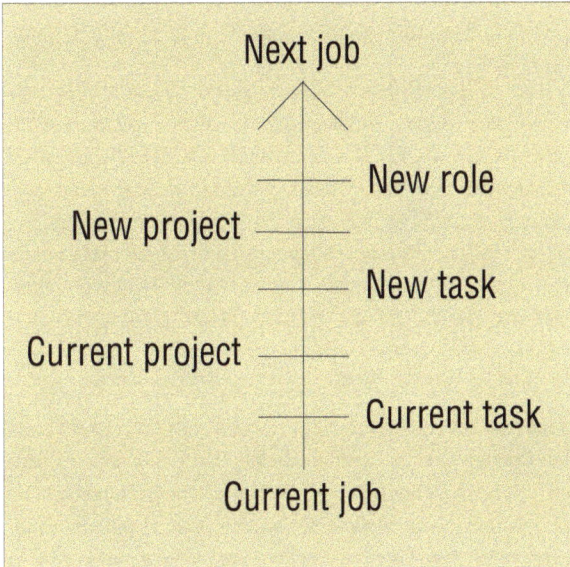

Exercise: 'mine' for an OTJ development opportunity

Purpose

To make you more aware of various OTJ development opportunities that exist close to home. This is ideally jointly done between a supervisor and each individual employee, but individuals can do it for their own jobs, too – and this includes you!

Instructions

Think you have all the experience that you need or that there's no opportunity for you to learn from your current role? 'Mine' your own job to identify an OTJ development opportunity that you are not currently aware of.

Long-term career development

It could be argued that many organisations have always supported staff career development. Isn't the requirement to complete an Individual Development Plan (IDP) or Performance Development Plan (or whatever it's called at your workplace) evidence of this? Yet, we know that, for many employers, the IDP isn't taken seriously. If it were, we'd see it referred to more often in promotion and placement decisions. How many have taken the time to flesh out the form, including our spoken languages, mobility preferences, etc., only to never be proactively identified for internal job openings based on any of this data?

Organisations with performance cultures take long-term career development seriously and appreciate that employees do have aspirations. So, although there are never any guarantees, they not only provide developmental support, they also expect staff to reflect on their career aspirations and have a career plan in place.

8. Designing a simple and minimal management process

Keep it simple

Organisations with strong performance cultures appreciate that the most important aspects of performance management are the essential elements (*see* page 2) – and not the process 'mechanics'. Sure, there are some decisions you need to make about how you set goals, offer feedback and make performance-related decisions, but don't over-engineer them. Employers make a mistake of placing too much emphasis on administrative and process matters – it may be apocryphal, but apparently employers make changes to their performance management processes every three years on average. It's as if they're searching for the Holy Grail: they're looking for a perfect performance management system that will never be found.

In building your performance culture, keep it simple. Aim for just enough process to allow the three essential elements to be realised. Aim for a process that lets performance flourish, not one that managers and staff have to workaround to do their jobs. Any time a process change is considered, ask these questions:

- Will it add any value?

- Will it help in setting goals or get in the way?
- Will it support the giving of meaningful feedback or get in the way?
- Will it improve how we identify how well our people are performing or just get in the way?

This chapter addresses a number of process aspects that you will need to consider:

- Rating scales
- Number of ratings
- Check-in and review formats
- Documentation

Rating scales

The history of performance management could easily equate to the progressive development of different types of rating scales to prevent error and bias by those doing the rating. However, after all those years and years of research, the general finding is that whichever rating scale format you choose doesn't make a great deal of difference.

So let's keep this simple: the one principle you should follow is to use *behaviourally anchored rating scales (BARS)*. Individual performance is best judged through observation of what people do, because behaviour is concrete and observable. BARS use behavioural definitions to anchor each rating point. You simply compare what was observed with each rating point. It's recommended starting at the mid-point as most people are average. If all the behaviour noted was observed, then you move up to the next scale point; if not, you move down to the next scale point.

Number of ratings

Don't worry about the number of points on your rating scale. They tend to proliferate because of the increasing desire to differentiate. Remember the 144-point scale that Google once used? (Engineers love quantitative data.) Five- and seven-point scales are now the most common. Some managers will tell you that the seven-point scale allows for greater differentiation. Yet, adding scale points doesn't add any value. It tends to be about personal preference.

Follow these simple principles on what number of rating points to use:

- If there's a lot at stake in terms of performance-related decisions (such as big bonuses), then a five-point scale is necessary to differentiate performance. I wouldn't go any higher.
- If performance is easy to measure quantitatively and there are obvious over-performers, but almost everybody else is 'satisfactory', stick with a three-point scale.

Check-in and review formats

Check-ins are a common element of many organisations' performance management refresh attempts. They are intended to be regular one-on-one sessions between manager and staff, and are usually scheduled.

Check-in formats vary, but generally provide an opportunity for manager and direct report to touch base on current work. From the employee's point of view, it's the time to report on what they are working on, their progress and any support needed. From the manager's perspective, it's the chance to have a regular view of the employee's work; it also allows the opportunity to offer support and resources.

Depending on how they're designed, check-ins may or may not include feedback. If they do, the intention is to offer *summary feedback* of what's being reviewed. A check-in should not be confused with real-time feedback. Remember, as described in Chapter 5, *real-time feedback* is feedback in the moment, right when it's needed. The focus should be on what's going on in that moment, there and then. Your intent is either to offer behavioural guidance on corrective action or on something done well, so the employee learns from and/or is motivated by the feedback. This can't wait for a scheduled check-in.

The structure of check-ins can take any form. In some workplaces, there will be no structure at all; managers and staff are just instructed to focus on whatever is relevant. Some workplaces will simply resort to the *traditional review format*: 'How are you getting on with your objectives? What's been achieved so far? Here's some feedback – what I've seen and what others have told me since we last spoke.' *Sandwich feedback* – with negative feedback preceded and followed by positive feedback – would be fitting here, if summary feedback is the intention. Increasingly common are the future-focus and strengths-based formats (*see* Chapter 5).

What type of check-in format, focus or structure would be most suited for a performance culture? This depends on what you are trying to achieve, but any structure would offer some guidance and sense of security for managers who might otherwise flounder over what to discuss. If the intent is to conduct a review, the conversation can be focused on objectives, progress and revision. If you want to emphasise values, the discussion could centre on examples of where the employee had exhibited (or not) the core values. Development and career growth could also be discussed, although be wary of raising this every time during frequent check-ins; career progression and development discussions take time, so artificially introducing the subjects into every conversation can misfire. Instead, take a lead from any milestones in place and review those that are upcoming or just past.

> ### Example: Kelly Services' twice-yearly discussions
>
> The American recruitment agency Kelly Services had a performance management process entitled 'My career'. Ongoing performance and development conversations are expected to occur throughout the year. Additionally, two formal meetings are held at different times of the year. In January, the meeting has a performance focus. Here manager and employee review and close old business goals, establish new ones and review development goal progress. In July, the focus is on development. The two parties review and close the current development plan, establish a new one and review business goal progress. Note how each conversation has a link to the other via reviews on business and development goal progress.

Check-ins can be as frequent as weekly (e.g. Deloitte), but the most common time period appears to be monthly (e.g. Gap) and some are quarterly. What should you do? The dynamic nature of your work context will dictate the frequency of check-ins. The more changeable and dynamic your environment, the more frequently reviews are needed. If the pace of progress and change are slower, then less frequent ones will suffice – possibly even just twice a year or annually – because real-time feedback fills the gaps. The risk with scheduling check-ins too frequently is that they become viewed as bureaucratic. So a strong recommendation is to encourage you to have check-ins only as really needed.

With more frequent touching base, is there still a need for an annual review? Keep in mind the purpose of this review: it is a comprehensive assessment of progress towards objectives, plus summary feedback. If you believe this is addressed amply through regular check-ins, omit the annual review.

Documentation

To simplify performance management processes, organisations are either reducing administrative requirements or completely eliminating required documentation around the performance review. If the latter, the performance review conversation does not need to be tracked or recorded. No forms or complicated paraphernalia are required. If elimination of performance ratings is involved, then this makes all the more sense. An example of this can be found at Kelly Services, where managers and their employees meet individually twice yearly to discuss performance and development, respectively, but they are not required to document what goes on in the sessions.

Keep in mind what would happen in a performance culture – the focus there is on the quality of the performance conversation, so any documentation would only be in place to support goal achievement. If in doubt about what and how much to document, ask these questions:

- What is essential?
- Will adding this requirement add any value or help goal achievement?
- Conversely, will this create an obstacle to goal achievement?

Some industries and governments may be required to have documentation of performance processes – but it is worth checking if this is more perception than actual requirement!

Agility

Simplification in itself can aid agility, but it's also important to ensure that the spirit of flexibility is built into any process. With ever-increasing change in the workplace, the old, once-a-year setting of performance objectives and performance review is no longer viable in many organisations. Performance cultures allow and encourage revisiting of objectives not just at check-ins, but when they *need* to be revisited. This may be due to early goal achievement or a change in context or priorities. So agility in shifting quickly to new goals and in new directions is essential and may involve setting shorter-term goals in the first place.

"

We all need people who will give us
feedback. That's how we improve.

Bill Gates

"

9. Building manager capability: manager as a catalyst

The central role of people managers should be evident in nearly all the other components of a performance culture described in the previous chapters. They:

- help make the corporate vision meaningful for their team and connect individuals to it

- set clear expectations for performance excellence (essential element 1)

- offer meaningful, useful feedback at the right moments (essential element 2)

- encourage flexing and adapting of objectives to changing situations

- make accurate distinctions between performance and appropriately reward different levels, including effectively managing under-performance (essential element 3)

- proactively leverage development opportunities through work experience and provide support for employees.

In many workplaces, a factor that might limit managers from taking on these roles is the excuse that there's too much to do 'in the day job'. In organisations with a culture of performance excellence, managers take on these roles as *part* of their day jobs – they are not add-ons. For example, Cargill (the massive, global provider of food, agriculture, financial and industrial products and services) entitles its performance management initiative *Everyday Performance Management* because it's part of what managers should be doing day to day. Google's Project Oxygen (*see* below) provides proof that it's such roles or managerial behaviours that allow teams to be successful.

Example: Google's Project Oxygen

Google wanted to understand the role of the people manager in teams' success. The question generating the Project Oxygen research project was whether people managers were necessary. Google's results found that highly effective managers' teams exhibited better performance, retention and work attitudes. The most impactful managerial behaviours related to coaching, empowerment, focus on staff success and well-being and a results orientation. For managers who insist on placing their professional/ functional tasks and roles before their managerial responsibilities, it's interesting to see that technical skills, while still important, were the least important of relevant managerial behaviours.

Any manager who embodies the above roles is a true *catalyst*. To be a catalyst is to be able to transform good performers into excellent ones, and even to help top performers realise additional potential. A catalyst is an exceptional boss who raises the bar and demands excellence.

Finding managers of this ilk is a tall order as they are quite rare. Organisations with a performance culture, however, select and grow their people managers to be performance catalysts. If your people managers are not yet acting in this way, not to worry – you can develop their capability. The focus is all on behaviours: setting expectations; being more flexible; giving constructive feedback; praising; rewarding; leveraging OTJ development; and being open to feedback themselves.

Engendering openness and trust

For these catalyst behaviours to operate effectively, there are two conditions: there must be trust between manager and staff, and there must be a culture of open communication. Ensuring that these two conditions are in place is often a challenge, especially in a workplace where transparency is not the norm. However, every people manager has within their control the capacity to be authentic and genuine when relating to their teams. Trust and open communication and the catalyst behaviours exist in a virtuous circle – each drives the others. For example, trust will engender acceptance of feedback, and accurate, constructive feedback will, in turn, encourage trust.

Managers in performance cultures do not hide behind excuses of what they cannot do because of having their 'hands tied' by upper management or a bureaucracy. Performance management guru Elaine Pulakos of PDRI explains that trust and open communication are enhanced when managers:

- explain what they know, what they don't know and what cannot yet be communicated – they verify their team's understanding
- keep their team informed and up to date

- make realistic commitments they can honour, and follow through – they do what they say they will. They explain their actions. They admit their limits and what they cannot do, upfront.

- show support for their team, regardless of what the issue is and how it might impact the team and other individuals. Where there is a genuine win–win, they highlight this – but they don't sugarcoat something that has no silver lining.

- communicate consistent principles of open communication and trust.

10. Bringing about cultural change

This book is about creating a culture of performance excellence. For many organisations, this means a significant change in how they currently approach performance management, meaning significant *cultural change*. This chapter is an introduction to the core aspects of this change – a sort of 'Cultural Change 101'. It is not a guide to how to undergo such a change; that would require a whole book on its own. We will cover making the case for change, change roles and the importance of embedding and reinforcing your new performance culture.

Make the case for change

People tend to resist change. You've heard it before: 'Better the devil you know.' The *change equation* below states that three factors must be present for meaningful change to occur:

$$D \times V \times F > R$$

D = *Dissatisfaction* with the *current state* – how things are now. This means that there has to be dissatisfaction with the existing performance management system or approach. This can be anything that makes people uncomfortable with the process. Without dissatisfaction, there's little motivation to change. Stakeholders must be convinced that the pain of not changing is likely to be greater than the uncertainty of change.

V = Vision of what is possible – a desirable *future state*. The proposed solution must be beneficial and free from the pain of the current state. People need to understand what is possible. If they don't have a clear vision of what things will be like after the change and why things will be better, they probably won't support the change. The clearer and more detailed you make this vision, the more likely it is that others will want to support the change.

F = First, concrete and practical steps that can be taken towards the vision – this is a roadmap or blueprint for change. Others must be convinced that the change is realistic and do-able. If viewed as too challenging, the possibility of change will seem remote. A 'future state' vision for change without a roadmap is just a frustrating bluster of hot air... which people will ignore.

If the product of these three factors is greater than...

R = Resistance, then change is possible.

Because D, V, and F are multiplied, if any one factor is absent (i.e. zero) or weak, then the product will be zero or low and therefore not capable of overcoming any resistance.

Resistance to change includes:

* people's limiting beliefs specific to that change – 'I don't see how any process with supervisory ratings can be fair.'
* general stubbornness or reluctance to change – 'I'm not willing to change.'
* general inertia or lack of interest – 'I can't be bothered to change.'

Any prior history of performance management approaches in the organisation should be acknowledged. If your organisation is like many others and has tinkered every so often with its performance management process – a new form here, a required conversation structure there – your employees may view any new changes with scepticism. 'I've seen all this before' is likely to be at the forefront of their minds. Remember this when making the case for change.

When making any change, there is usually a range of *stakeholders*, and each stakeholder group may have different motivations for change. For instance, the case for change is typically a business one, especially to gain the support of executives. The business case might be to achieve greater strategic alignment, greater employee engagement leading to increased productivity, or reduced administrative costs due to a simplified approach. But also remember that you may need to appeal on a more emotional level to everyone who is not in an executive role.

Top tip: making the case for change

Making the case for change involves preparation. Focus first on the *current state*: How did we get here? What's not working? You'll need to make an urgent case, so draw on your strongest evidence: use or create data and collect stories that depict the pain of the current state. For example, what percentage of staff are dissatisfied with the current performance management approach? What impact does it have on employee engagement? What are the costs and how will we suffer if it continues? The ultimate message is suffused with gloom for everyone involved, unless action is taken.

Next, turn to the *future state*. What would an improved performance management approach consist of? What are the benefits of moving to this state? You can also get creative here, to help stakeholders visualise a better place. Imagine the future: What does it look, feel, sound like? What are the potential outcomes, such as: 'Morale will improve by...' and

'Productivity will increase by...'? Think about a headline that you'd like to appear in the financial news a year from now – what does it say about your organisation's transformation?

Finally, consider the *first steps* of your change process. What are some practical, concrete actions that will reflect a move towards the new performance management approach? While you may not be prepared with a fully developed approach, your aim is to show stakeholders that the future state is possible and within reach.

Change roles

In the previous section, the term *stakeholder* was used; this refers to a person with an interest in or concern about something. In this case, stakeholder refers to someone who will experience the change in question. Most stakeholders in this situation will be the *targets* of this change, meaning that they will experience the change as happening *to* them – hence, why resistance to change is so common. How would you feel if something were being done to you? It's important to keep an image of both employees and managers as targets; to remember that they may feel as if they're not in control of what's happening to and around them. Also keep in mind that different stakeholders/ targets may have different concerns and motivations for resisting change. Therefore, different aspects of the future state may actually appeal to them.

At the other end of the spectrum is the *change champion* or *sponsor*. Typically, this is a senior executive like the managing director or CEO. This is arguably the *most* important role, because this is the figurehead or leader of the desired change. The change champion leads the change by virtue of their status and influence. They bring authority, resources and accountability. They have the power to enact change.

An effective sponsor fronts the change, leads it, drives it, 'walks the talk' and marshals others towards it. Their focus is on the desirable future state. If they don't act as a role model for the change, then others will not follow.

As a figurehead, the sponsor should not be too burdened with the detail and elaborate preparation that goes into careful change management. Instead, they empower a *change agent* to facilitate change. The change agent doesn't have any authority to bring about change or make things transpire; they simply manage and coordinate the planning that goes into the change initiative. This means working closely with the sponsor, coaching them on how to act (e.g. as a role model) and what to say regarding the change initiative.

Embedding and reinforcing a performance culture

Organisational cultures don't just form on their own. The most senior leaders create them through their status and influence. They determine what is important, what gets done and what gets rewarded. They determine the core values. Most of the time, culture creation isn't such a conscious act; instead, people observe, consciously and unconsciously, what senior leaders do and how they behave, and they follow. However, even with this in mind, building a culture of performance excellence still requires some conscious effort. There are three mechanisms to plan and manage this: communication; education; and reinforcement.

Communication

When introducing an important change, in order for people to understand and accept it, you have to tell them what's coming, tell them what is happening and let them know what has just happened. In other words, you can never communicate enough. Change communication must be strategic and planned. A *communication plan* is a formal means of ensuring that communication is strategic. It comprehensively addresses all aspects of change communication, leaving nothing to chance.

Phase: Change initiatives occur in three major phases – current state (now), future state (the desirable potential future) and delta state (the chaos ensuing in between). Communication during each phase is vital, especially during the delta state, as people start to grapple with the change and become stressed by what is unfolding.

Stakeholders: Who do we need to communicate with? Different stakeholders will have different concerns, so one size does *not* fit all. There may need to be multiple messaging about the same change aspect, related in different ways.

Message content: What information do we want to convey? Whatever the message, ensure these key points are addressed from the perspective of the stakeholder group in question:

- How is this relevant to what you do?
- What should you do? What is being asked of you?
- What does success/failure look like?
- What tools and support will be available?
- What's in it for you?

Media: What form of communication is most apt for this stakeholder group and this message, at this time? Options include

Figure 8 A communication plan

Phase	Stake-holders	Mesage content	Media	Ownership	Timing
Current state	VPs	Morale problems with performance appraisal, including survey data	Face-to-face executive meeting	HR to present, with sponsor-ship from CEO	February monthly meeting
Current state	People managers	Notice of intention to modify Performance Appraisal, request for further input	Email, followed by department meetings	HR and functional VPs	March – April
Delta state	Employees	Transition to new approach will take time; training roll-out for all will take time. Offer of 'clin-ics' to voice concerns about process and managerial resistance.	Email, followed by town hall sessions for all staff	HR and functional VPs	Early May

email, teleconference, team or department/division meetings, and larger town hall sessions.

Ownership: Who is responsible for driving this communication? The change agent may help craft many communications, but ownership typically is by sponsors or a relevant function, depending on the message (e.g. a performance management process change may come from both the CEO and HR).

Timing: When should a message or communication occur?

Top tip: communication checklist

Recommendation	Reasoning
Repeat the message over and over	We're inundated with communication and cope by screening things out; this ensures the message is received at least once.
Vary the medium	We may not see or hear the message in one format, but will via another.
Communicate both ways – listen!	People are more receptive to engaging in a topic, rather than just being told what to do. Genuinely listen to stakeholders' concerns.
First, understand...	Do stakeholders know what is involved? Explain the change first, before seeking agreement.
Consider timing	What else is going on that might distract your stakeholders? Is there a best time during the day or week to send your message?

Act consistently with messaging	People look for clues in how leaders actually behave. If your message is inconsistent with how the change's sponsor would communicate, this implies dishonesty and shenanigans – any sign of this, and staff will get an inkling of a hidden, unintended message.
Tell the truth, both the good and the bad	People recognise sugar coating and when something is being withheld; they then hear only balderdash and 'management speak'. If you can't announce specifics, communicate as much as you can honestly.

Education

If communication consists of informing stakeholders about *what's* happening (or about to happen or has happened), education is about teaching them *how* to comply with any new requirements. It's one thing to announce what is different; it's another to skill-up targets with relevant behaviours.

Just what needs to be taught will depend upon the change involved. In building performance cultures, enhancing managerial capability is essential; typically, managers lack the necessary behavioural skills. So it's very common for organisations to provide managers with training in feedback and coaching skills, performance assessment and the performance management process itself. By deciding on additional relevant skills to be honed, those in charge of change are setting clear expectations, linking reward to performance, carrying out performance calibration within and across teams, and devising appropriate performance documentation suitable to the context. Employers should appreciate that employees will also need some skill building in how to ask for feedback and receive it, as well as offering feedback to colleagues and upwards to their bosses.

Reinforcement

As noted earlier, the most senior leaders have the status and influence to shape a performance culture... or, conversely, to create a culture that accepts mediocrity. Because of what they say and do, others follow. Well-known organisational development expert Edgar Schein says that leaders primarily embed a new culture by:

- 'unfreezing' the current state by highlighting organisational threats if no change occurs, while making others believe that change is possible and desirable
- articulating a new direction and a new set of assumptions – they act as deliberate role models
- vetting how people should behave, by rewarding new behaviours and punishing old ones, including creating 'critical incidents' that others see and are aware of.

So, in establishing a clear performance culture, it's vital that leaders (and managers at all levels) more consciously consider their actions and words. Here are various ways in which managers and leaders can proactively shape the new culture:

- Engage staff in dialogue about the performance culture: talk openly about what is expected and what 'good' looks like.
- 'Walk the(ir) talk' and role model the behaviour they want to see in others.
- Measure and reward exactly what is expected – e.g. identify supervisors known for giving effective feedback and 'put them on show'.

- Invest resources (money, people, time) in a performance culture – fully integrate principles of performance excellence throughout the organisation, not just in random dribs and drabs.

In addition to the day-to-day behaviours of leaders and managers, there are 'secondary mechanisms' to reinforce a performance culture. These can have both a practical and symbolic purpose: practical in that something is literally achieved – a process or communication – but symbolic in what the mechanisms represent. These include:

- *organisational systems and procedures*, such as a performance management process that identifies what is important by what must be actioned and what gets measured. For example, a simple and agile process reflects the value of the performance discussion, not the process. Also, regular evaluation – such as an employee survey asking about manager proactivity regarding real-time feedback and quality of feedback – can be a powerful incentive.

- *organisational rites and rituals*, such as expected real-time feedback and check-ins. You could also launch an 'enhancement rite' to represent the value of good feedback – say, a ceremony during which awards for the best feedback givers or 'development opportunity miners' are given.

- *stories* that embody what a performance culture looks and feels like. Typically stories are communicated ad hoc – e.g. leaders may recount stories informally as they deal with different challenges day to day. They also can be skilfully integrated into formal communications, such as presentations and in the 'About Us' section on the corporate website.

- *formal statements* of organisational philosophy and values around performance excellence. The starting place is the organisation's vision and mission statements, and then high-lighted at meaningful junctures like new hire induction and team-building sessions. It's also a strategic move to promi-nently place such detail on the corporate website, so that like-minded job applicants are attracted.

Example: reinforcing your performance culture through secondary means

Purpose

To help you plan how, in a practical way, you can build per-formance culture reinforcement mechanisms into everyday work practices and processes.

Instructions

After considering the secondary mechanisms listed above, have a think about what you could design in your organ-isation to help reinforce a performance culture. Think both practically and symbolically. Produce a list of systems and processes, activities, communications and other means. Consider what each might look like in implementation – for-mal or informal, concrete or less tangible, time required, any costs, leadership and staff involvement (and who leads or directs the activity), intended objectives, etc. When you've fleshed this out somewhat, take it to your leadership team and discuss what you'd like to implement and how you would proceed.

Further reading

Aguinis, H. and O'Boyle, E. (2012). The best and the rest: Revisiting the norm of normality of individual performance. *Personnel Psychology*, *65*(1), 79–119.

CEB. (May 2016). Removing performance ratings is unlikely to improve performance. Survey of 9500 employees and 300 HR managers.

Globoforce (2012). Workforce Mood Tracker Fall 2012 report: Revealing key practices for effective recognition. http://go.globoforce.com/rs/globoforce/images/Fall_Mood tracker_2012Survey_web.pdf

Graham, G. H. and Unruh, J. (1990). The motivational impact of non-financial employee appreciation practices on medical technologists. *Health Care Supervisor*, *8*(3), 9–17.

Grote, D. (2011). *How to be good at performance appraisals*. Harvard Business Review Press.

Haydon, John (accessed April 2017). 30 example mission statements. *TopNonprofits*: https://topnonprofits.com/examples/vision-statements/

Ledford, G., Benson, G. and Lawler, E. (August 2016). Cutting-edge performance management: 244 organisations report on ongoing feedback, ratingless reviews, and crowd-sourced feedback. WorldatWork Research.

McCall, M. W., Lombardo, M. M. and Morrison, A. N. (1988). *Lessons of experience: How successful executives develop on the job*. Lexington, MA: Lexington Books.

Meyers, M. C., van Woerkom, M., de Reuver, R., Bakk, Z. and Oberski, D. L. (2015). Enhancing psychological capital and personal growth initiative: Working on strengths or deficiencies? *Journal of Counselling Psychology*, *62*(1), 50–62.

Pulakos, E. D. (2009). *Performance management: A new approach for driving business results*. Wiley-Blackwell.

Schein, E. H. (2010). *Organizational culture and leadership*. Jossey-Bass.

About the author

Gene is an evidence-based work psychologist who is passionate about helping organisations prosper and individuals achieve their full potential.

Trained in the scientist-practitioner model, he acts as a trusted advisor to employers on how to facilitate and enhance business and individual performance. This means that he applies 'science' (theory and research) to practical, day-to-day challenges in the workplace. This may involve selecting leaders or identifying high potential staff through psychometrics, structured interviews, and other valid tools; helping executives 'walk their talk' in building a culture of performance excellence; or guiding managers in how to more skilfully utilise employee engagement levers. Whatever the application, Gene's clients can be sure that the tools and techniques involved will be evidence-based and robust.

Gene has worked in academia, government, consultancy and the corporate sector. He has lived and worked in the US, New Zealand, Australia, Germany and the UK. He is the Managing Director of Working Matters, a work psychology and management consultancy operating in the UK, Asia Pacific and internationally.

THE
AUTHORITY
GUIDES

We hope that you've enjoyed reading this *Authority Guide*. Titles in this series are designed to offer highly practical and easily-accessible advice on a range of business, leadership and management issues.

We're always looking for new authors. If you're an expert in your field and are interested in working with us, we'd be delighted to hear from you. Please contact us at commissioning@suerichardson.co.uk and tell us about your idea for an *Authority Guide*.

EU Safety Representative: euComply OÜ Pärnu mnt 139b-14 11317 Tallinn
Estonia hello@eucompliancepartner.com +33 756 90241

www.ingramcontent.com/pod-product-compliance
Lightning Source LLC
Chambersburg PA
CBHW061052200326
41520CB00027BA/7520